Butterflies

Dee White

Here is a butterfly.

Butterflies have a small body.
They have big wings.

Butterflies can fly.
They go from flower to flower.

This butterfly is on the flower.

Butterflies look for food.

The food is in the flowers.
It is called nectar.

There are all kinds of butterflies.
Some butterflies look like flowers.

Some butterflies look like trees.

Some butterflies have lots of colours.

This butterfly has two colours.
It is red and black.

Butterflies cannot fly when they are cold.

The sun makes them warm.
Then they can fly!

Butterflies hide at night.
They rest on leaves.

Butterflies do not go to sleep.

Look at these butterflies.
They are beautiful!